Advance Praise for

AUSCHWITZ EXPLAINED
TO MY CHILD

"THIS IS AN important addition to Holocaust
education literature. Writing concisely with
intelligence and dignity, Annette Wieviorka
educates the reader about the Holocaust by
answering haunting questions about the mass
murder of the European Jews posed to her by
her own daughter. Her answers, and her
daughter's questions, will inform not only
children but adults as well. I will urge my
own children to read it."

—ERIC A. JOHNSON,
Professor of History and author of
*Nazi Terror: The Gestapo, Jews,
and Ordinary Germans*

"WITHOUT TALKING DOWN to her readers,
Wieviorka directly answers those questions
about the Holocaust that young people
most frequently ask."

—SUSAN BACHRACH,
author of *Tell Them We Remember:
The Story of the Holocaust*

AUSCHWITZ

Explained to My Child

Annette Wieviorka

FOREWORD BY
Peter Hellman

TRANSLATED BY
Leah Brumer

MARLOWE & COMPANY
NEW YORK

AUSCHWITZ EXPLAINED TO MY CHILD

Copyright © Éditions du Seuil, 1999
Translation Copyright © Leah Brumer 2002
Foreword Copyright © Peter Hellman 2002

Published by
Marlowe & Company
An Imprint of Avalon Publishing Group Incorporated
161 William Street, 16th Floor
New York, NY 10038

First published as *Auschwitz expliqué à ma fille* by Éditions
du Seuil in France in 1999. This edition published by
arrangement with Éditions du Seuil.

Library of Congress Cataloging-in-Publication Data
is available.

9 8 7 6 5 4 3 2 1

Paperback ISBN 1-56924-552-5
Hardcover ISBN 1-56924-516-9

Designed by Pauline Neuwirth, Neuwirth & Associates, Inc.

Printed in Canada
Distributed by Publishers Group West

•

To my daughter, Mathilde
To my nieces, Sophie, Éve, Elsa, and Nadia

CONTENTS

FOREWORD

Sometimes it takes a simple marker to bring home the reality of something complicated. Mathilde, who asks the questions in this brief but important book, knew that her mom's friend, Berthe, was a survivor of the Auschwitz death camp. But it wasn't until the 13-year-old French girl saw the number tattooed in "faded blue" on Berthe's forearm that the reality of Auschwitz hit home. Yes, there really had been a place where thousands of people became numbers. And, as Mathilde learns from her mom, they were the lucky ones. Almost a million other men, women and children became ashes. Among them were three of Mathilde's great grandparents.

I know the shock that Mathilde felt, seeing that tattoo on Berthe's left forearm. Each time I visit my friend Helen in her New York apartment, a cheerful old woman who likes flowered dresses, I'm also shocked each and every time I see the tattoo on her chubby arm. Her number, 2286, makes Auschwitz more real to me than the place itself, which I've visited three times. But if you have no clue of what happened at Auschwitz, such a tattoo will be meaningless. Or worse, lead you to a wrong conclusion. Another survivor, named Lili, once told me of an incident that occurred soon after she immigrated to this country with her new husband. They were trying to rent an apartment in Miami when the rental agent noticed Lili's Auschwitz tattoo.

"Can't you even remember your own telephone number without writing it on your arm?" the agent asked. Had he read the read the book in your hands, he'd have never asked such an ignorant question.

As a teenager, I read a newspaper story that, even though it was not even on the front page, struck me as terribly important. It reported the death of a very old African-American woman who had been the last surviving person born a slave in the South. It seemed momentous that nobody was left to talk about slavery in the first person. After her, it was all dry history in print.

If you're now a teenager or in your early twenties, the time will come before middle age that you'll read—on line, probably, not in a newspaper—a story that will be just as momentous as the one I saw as a teenager. It will report the death of the last person who survived Auschwitz, the last to bear a death camp tattoo, the last to be able to say, "I was there, and yes, one group of human beings really did do this to another group."

When that day comes, I hope you'll know more about Auschwitz than I knew about slavery. Paying attention to Mathilde's questions and her mom's answers will help you to be that knowledgeable person.

PETER HELLMAN is the author of *When Courage Was Stronger Than Fear: Remarkable Stories of Christians Who Saved Jews from the Holocaust,* and he wrote the text for *The Auschwitz Album: A Book Based Upon an Album Discovered By a Concentration Camp Survivor, Lili Meier.* He lives in New York City.

INTRODUCTION

I N THE SUMMER of 1999, when we were at
the beach on vacation, we met Berthe, a
friend of mine. Around ten years ago, she and I
became close when I was working on an oral
history project related to the Holocaust. I had
interviewed her about being deported to the
concentration camp Auschwitz–Birkenau. We're
in touch now almost every week, even if just by
phone. We often talk about news related to the
genocide of the Jews during World War II, like
the 1997 trial of Maurice Papon, a Frenchman
who collaborated with the Germans, or Roberto
Benigni's 1998 movie, *Life is Beautiful.*

That summer my daughter, Mathilde, was 13.
She knew Berthe and that she'd been a prisoner
at Auschwitz. If Berthe called and I wasn't home,
Mathilde often took her phone messages. But
Mathilde was still shocked to see a faded number

tattooed in blue ink on Berthe's arm. In one harsh moment, everything Mathilde had heard at home, on television, in the movies, or at school came to life and became real. Suddenly, the Holocaust became real.

A few years ago Mathilde had to draw her family tree for an elementary school project. She had known her four grandparents but it was difficult to find information on the exact date and place of her great-grandparents' deaths. On her father's side, Rywka Raczymow had died at Auschwitz. On my side, so had Roza and Wolf Wieviorka. The Germans killed Mathilde's maternal great-grandmother, Chawa Perelman, near Chalon-sur-Saône after the July 16, 1942 round-up of Jews at the Vélodrome d'Hiver, the Paris sports arena. She had been trying to cross from occupied France into the free zone. Uncles and aunts were murdered, too, but they didn't appear on the tree.

Mathilde's father and I were named after relatives who died at Auschwitz. Are we still prisoners of that legacy? We've experienced this painful history indirectly and have tried to come to terms with it in our work. He is a writer and I am an historian. At 13, Mathilde had to be aware of the Holocaust. We talked about it in the family and with friends. At home, books and magazines on the subject were everywhere. She had heard me talk about it on radio and television. Yet she'd never really asked any questions. I'd never really had to explain.

When I did try to explain Auschwitz to Mathilde, it struck me that her questions were the ones I've been asking myself forever. They are the same ones that have haunted philosophers and historians for a half-century. She just asked them bluntly and directly.

AUSCHWITZ
Explained to My Child

E VEN IF IT'S easy for me to describe Auschwitz and explain how the genocide of the Jews took place, there's still something deeper that's impossible to understand and explain: Why did the Nazis want to rid the planet of Jews? Why were they so zealous in combing the four corners of the continent they occupied, from Amsterdam to Bordeaux, from Warsaw to Thessaloniki, looking for children and old people—just to murder them?

Why does Berthe have that number tattooed on her arm?

The number you saw was tattooed on Berthe's arm in Auschwitz. She was deported during World War II. That means she was taken against her will from the country where she lived, France, to another country, Poland.

When we talk about World War II "deportees," we mean they ended up in concentration camps.

Why do you say Berthe was taken to Poland?

Because the Auschwitz camp was in Poland.

*What happened to Berthe? It's strange—
I've known her forever but I don't really
know anything about her.*

On July 16, 1942, Berthe was arrested in Paris. That day French police, following orders from the Germans, arrested nearly 13,000 Jews. Families with children were held in a huge arena that used to host bicycle races and political rallies. It was called the Vélodrome d'Hiver, the Winter Sports Arena. That's why we call the arrest of all those people the Vél d'Hiv round-up.

What's a round-up?

It's a mass arrest the police conduct without warning. The sports arena has been torn down but every year there's a ceremony so we won't forget what happened there. At the time,

Berthe was 19 years old and single. She wasn't sent to the arena. Instead, like other single people and childless couples, she was taken by bus to a camp near Paris, in Drancy.

Was Drancy a concentration camp?

Yes, if you think of a concentration camp as a place where people are held and deprived of their freedom. But Drancy didn't look like the Nazi camps. When Berthe was there, it was a transit camp. People stayed for just a little while before being deported. Berthe was there for about two weeks. Then she was taken, again by bus, to a little train station nearby in Bobigny. She and several thousand other people were made to board a freight car. They rode the train for three days and three nights. It was summer. Men, women, and children were stuffed into the car. The heat was horrible and they had nothing to eat or drink. You could go crazy just from thirst. Some people did go mad. Then the train arrived at another little station. It was called Oswiecim in Polish and Auschwitz in German. Those names didn't mean anything then.

Why were there two names for the same place?

In 1939, the Nazis annexed the province of
Upper Silesia, which at that time was a far-off
area of southern Poland. They gave German
names to all the Polish places.

When the train doors opened, Berthe heard
voices yelling in German and dogs barking.
You've seen similar scenes in lots of movies.
Berthe had lived in Germany until 1933,
when she was 10. By then Hitler had come to
power so she knew what those noises and cries
meant. The passengers were ordered to move
quickly and leave their suitcases and packages
on the train platform. Men as thin as skeletons
scurried around them. The men's heads were
shaved and they wore clothes that looked like
striped pajamas.

The Germans announced that people who
were tired could go to the camp in trucks.
They separated the new arrivals into two
groups. People who were old or worn-out,
children and pregnant women boarded the
trucks. The others, including Berthe, left on
foot. Men and women were separated and sent
to different camps. Berthe was sent to the
women's camp at Birkenau, about 1½ miles
from the main camp at Auschwitz.

Then what happened to them?

The women had to undress. At that time, people were much more modest than they are today. You were never naked in front of someone else. This was the first humiliation they suffered. Even their most private places were searched and they were sent to the showers. Their heads, armpits, and genital area were shaved. They were given clothes—not the striped pajamas or dresses like you see in photos, war movies, or museums—but filthy, raggedy things. The Germans had taken these clothes from earlier deportees but decided they weren't worth keeping. Other detainees had already worn them. And then the Germans engraved an indelible number in their flesh, using a metal pen and blue ink. That's what you saw on Berthe's arm.

Did it hurt?

Many people have told me it didn't hurt very much. But it stripped them of their names, the last thing they had left. From then on they were called only by this number. They could never erase it. They had to repeat it in German every morning and night during roll call. Sometimes the roll call lasted for hours.

No one had anything left from life before the camps— not a single object, not a picture, not a piece of clothing. When the Italian writer Primo Levi got out of Auschwitz, he described his camp experiences in a book called *If This Is A Man*. You can read it. "Nothing belongs to us anymore," he wrote. "They have taken away our clothes, our shoes, even our hair . . . They will even take away our names: and if we want to keep them, we will have to find in ourselves the strength to do so, to manage somehow so that behind that name something of us, of us as we were, still remains."

They had entered a different world. That's how many of the survivors describe it. But Levi probably said it best: "Imagine now a man who is deprived not only of everyone he loves but at the same time of his house, his habits, his clothes, in short, of everything he possesses: he will be a hollow man, reduced to suffering and needs, forgetful of dignity and restraint, for he who loses all often easily loses himself. He will be a man whose life or death can be lightly decided with no sense of human kinship, on the basis of a pure judgment of his utility."

I didn't know Berthe was German
and that she'd had to leave her country in 1933
when Hitler came to power.

Yes, Berthe was German. Her family lived like other German families of the same social class. Her father was a doctor who worked in a hospital with his colleagues. When Hitler and his political party, the Nazi party, came to power they turned their hatred of Jews into action. Hitler's first goal was to separate Jews from other Germans. He wanted to cut their social and economic ties, one by one, to the country. From then on, people identified as Jews lost their jobs. They couldn't swim in public pools or go to theaters or concerts. Their children had to attend separate schools. But it was complicated. Of the 500,000 Jews who lived in Germany, only a few were religious. For them, being Jewish defined all aspects of daily life. Some were involved in Jewish political life. For example, they might have been Zionists, which means they wanted Jews to have their own country in the land of Palestine. That country, Israel, was created in 1948 after World War II. But the majority of Jews were completely assimilated. For them, being Jewish no longer meant anything. They didn't practice their religion or belong to

Jewish organizations. They didn't know anything about Judaism. Some German Jews, or their parents or grandparents, had even converted to Catholicism or Protestantism. Many had married non-Jews.

So if you weren't Jewish any more, you weren't in danger?

For Hitler, being Jewish meant you belonged to a "race." If your grandparents were Jewish, then you were Jewish whether you wanted to be or not, even if you had become Catholic.

In Hitler's vision of the world, this race had to disappear from the "greater Germany" he dreamed of building. All German-speaking countries, like Austria, would be part of this empire, even if it meant he had to declare war on them. He would conquer the Russians, Ukrainians, and Poles. He said Germany must be rid of Jews—*Judenfrei*, in German—or cleansed of Jews—*Judenrein*. Once that was accomplished, the Aryan race would take power for 1,000 years and the world would be reborn.

Were Jews able to get out of Germany?

Some, like those who lost their jobs or were victims of violence, did leave. That's how Berthe's parents came to France. You read Anne Frank's diary. Her family went to Amsterdam. Then in 1939 the war started and large areas of Europe were occupied. The Nazis had caught up with the Jews.

You said some Jews assimilated and that nothing set them apart from other Germans.

Yes, you're right. It is impossible to tell who is Jewish. In France, for example, until the French Revolution of 1789, things were pretty simple. To be Jewish meant following a tradition, a religious tradition that provided a structure for every aspect of social life. It defined the legal system, the calendar, marriage, and birth. So Jews formed a "nation" and lived apart from others. Later they were emancipated, meaning they were granted legal equality with non-Jews. They became citizens like everyone else.

While some Jews held on to their religious practices, others wanted to melt into the population of the countries where they lived. In principle, nothing set them apart from other Germans or other French people. At school, for example, you don't know who's Jewish unless your friends tell you, or if someone wears a Star of David or a yarmulke or observes the Sabbath as a day of rest.

So how did the Germans find out if someone was Jewish?

To identify someone as Jewish, the German administration first had to define whom it considered Jewish. This wasn't easy because there had been so many mixed marriages in Germany. All Germans had to prove that they didn't have any Jewish ancestors—that is, relatives who belonged to the Jewish religion and who hadn't been baptized either Protestant or Catholic. Sometimes they had to trace their family tree back to the seventeenth century. Next, the Germans ordered a census of Jews in every country they occupied: Austria first, in March 1938, and then Czechoslovakia, Poland, and France. In France, for example, they held the census two months after the Germans entered Paris on September 27, 1940. All Jews living in the occupied zone had to appear at their local police station if they lived in Paris, or at the

regional police headquarters if they lived
outside the city. Almost everyone showed up.

Why?

This is difficult to understand today, but it was
normal to be counted then because that was
the law. No one could have imagined what was
going to happen. We refer to France as a
nation of laws, a country with rules that
everyone must respect. French government
agencies were responsible for carrying out the
census and French Jews were citizens like
everyone else. If Jewish foreigners were living
in France, they enjoyed the protection of their
host country. Even if being Jewish didn't mean
anything anymore to some people, being
counted was a question of self-respect and
dignity. Take the philosopher Henri Bergson,
the first Jew elected to the French Academy.
He won the 1927 Nobel Prize in Literature.
He was Catholic in his heart although he had
not converted. Even so, he insisted on going to
his local police station in solidarity with Jews.
He was 80 and very ill. He died the next year.

What happened after the Jews were counted?

In the Seine region, which included Paris and
surrounding towns, 149,734 Jews (85,664
French and 64,070 foreign Jews) were
counted. Using the census forms the Jews
completed, the Germans instructed French
police to create four sets of files: by alpha-
betical order, profession, address, and
nationality. No one knew it then, but later
those files would be used to carry out arrests
and deportations.

In May 1941 the files were used for the first
time. The Germans decided to arrest foreign
Jewish men, especially Poles like your great-
grandparents. The men received a summons
ordering them to come to their local police
station. When they got to the station, they
were put on buses and taken to the Austerlitz
train station. From there, they traveled to two
camps in Pithiviers and Beaune-la-Rolande, in
the Loiret region not far from Orléans.

Arrests began again in August 1941 but the
procedure was different. Based on the
information in police files, the Germans
targeted the 11th *arrondissement,* or district, a
Paris neighborhood where many Jews lived.
Before daybreak, French police surrounded
the area. They went door-to-door all day long

looking for people. They arrested some on the street. Since they couldn't find everyone on their list, over the next five days the Germans and the French police arrested Jews from all over Paris. (By that time, many Jews had realized it wasn't safe to stay in occupied France and secretly crossed over into the free zone.) They only arrested men, but this time they didn't take just foreigners. French Jews were rounded up, too, including some prominent lawyers. As usual, they were taken by bus and sent to Drancy, the camp Berthe passed through a year later.

You said Drancy wasn't really a concentration camp.

Drancy didn't look like what you might imagine a concentration camp to be. It looked more like an unfinished housing project or apartment buildings where no one had ever lived. Several hundred apartments were divided among three buildings, which formed a U-shape around a big courtyard. The place certainly wasn't set up to house 4,000 men. In the beginning, the men weren't even allowed to send letters or receive packages. They had almost nothing to

eat and more than 30 died of hunger.
Imagine dying of hunger, even during the
war, in a country like France, where no one
had died of hunger in more than 100 years!
In December 1941, around 700 prominent
people—lawyers and army officers, the elite
of French society—were rounded up in a
smaller mass arrest.

So they arrested only men?

Yes. But everything changed with the terrible
Vél d'Hiv episode that I mentioned. Acting on
German orders, the French police arrested
13,000 people over two days. But this time
they took mostly women and children.
(Before, news of round-ups had leaked,
sometimes from police headquarters, which
gave men time to hide. But women and
children assumed they wouldn't be arrested so
they remained at home.) They were taken to
the sports arena, where they spent several
horrible days before being transferred to camps
in the Loiret region, at Pithiviers and Beaune-
la-Rolande. The men who'd been arrested in
May 1941 were gone by then. They had been
deported to Auschwitz. The mothers were
separated from their children. That was awful
to see. Then the women were deported.

Without their children?

The Germans hadn't yet arranged to deport children. But Pierre Laval, head of the French government, suggested they be deported, too. While the French waited for an answer from Berlin, the children stayed with social workers in the camps at Pithiviers and Beaune-la-Rolande. Then they were taken to Drancy and they, too, were put on trains.

Why?

When I told you about Berthe's trip, I said that when people arrived in Birkenau a few of them went on foot to the huts and most of the others got onto trucks. The trucks brought them to a group of unusual buildings. First, they were sent into a changing room, where they undressed. The changing room led into other rooms that looked like showers where a deadly gas, Zyklon B, was released from the ceiling. The gas asphyxiated them very quickly. Their bodies were taken out and burned in huge crematoriums. We usually call these buildings gas chambers, but sometimes we use the word crematorium. These were both. The building plans for these installations have been found. Some museums, like the one built at Auschwitz at the end of the war and the Holocaust Museum in Washington, D.C., have built models of the gas chambers.

Who did this work? The Germans?

People were divided up on the platforms in a process known as "the selection." Some, judged "fit for work," entered the camps. Others went straight to "the gas," as the prisoners called it. German doctors decided who would go where. The Germans also administered the deadly gas. But it was the prisoners, organized into what were called *Sonderkommando,* special commandos, who had to burn the bodies. They didn't have that job for very long because they, too, were gassed on a regular basis.

Why were they gassed if they were useful, fit for work?

So they would never tell anyone what they had seen and had been forced to do. The Germans didn't want anyone to know about what was going on.

Why did it have to be kept secret since all the Jews in the camp were going to die?

The Germans didn't want to draw attention to what was happening and they wanted the deportees to remain obedient. The *Sonderkommando*'s horrible job was a terrifying secret.

I realize that even as I do my best to explain this to you as clearly and calmly as possible, I'm not really explaining anything. Here I am talking about a technical procedure. How can I help you understand that no one had ever heard of anything like this? That despite the massacres that have occurred throughout history, no one had ever built anything like this—a factory with an assembly line set up to kill people? That at Birkenau alone, perhaps as many as one million people were killed on a tiny piece of ground?

Many people kept journals during that time. One of them, Abraham Lewin, lived in the Warsaw ghetto. He wrote of hearing a rumor that 10-year-old children in the ghetto of Lodz, another large Polish city, were being killed. "It is difficult for the tongue to pronounce such words, for the soul to understand their meaning, to put them on paper," he wrote in his journal.

You know, the death of a child is the most awful, devastating thing that can happen. In school you memorized the poem, "Tomorrow, at Dawn," by the French writer Victor Hugo. He wrote it four years after his daughter accidentally drowned. You were upset by his inconsolable grief. Children suffer and die in massacres and famine. But Auschwitz was different. Auschwitz was about attacking an entire people, reaching all the way to their descendants, tracking down their children wherever they were and murdering them so this group of people would disappear from the earth forever.

Sometimes you say Auschwitz,
sometimes Birkenau . . .

Auschwitz is the name of the main camp. The Nazis opened it after they conquered Poland. Members of the Polish opposition and elite like professors and priests were sent there. It was like the concentration camps the Nazis built in Germany after they seized power in 1933. They locked up people who had fought them—Socialists, Communists, and some Catholics—and used those arrests to terrorize the population. The first of these

concentration camps was built in Dachau, in
Germany. Buchenwald and the women's
camp, Ravensbruck, followed. In 1938, when
Austria was annexed to Germany, the Nazis
opened a camp there in Mauthausen. When
they annexed Alsace in 1940, they opened the
Struthof camp near Strasbourg. In Poland,
they built Auschwitz, which they set up in
brick buildings the army had used before. The
SS was in charge there.

What does SS mean?

SS are the German initials for *Schutzstaffel,*
which means "elite guard." At first they were
Hitler's personal bodyguards, a private police
force for him and the Nazi party. After the
Nazis took power, the group grew to about
250,000 men, although it was never really
large. They were completely indoctrinated and
violently anti-Semitic. Little by little, under
the direction of Hitler's most loyal follower,
Heinrich Himmler, they became like a state
within a state. They were responsible for
running the concentration camps and
eliminating Jews.

So Birkenau was a concentration camp, too?

Yes and no. The Nazis anticipated the attack
on the Soviet Union, which took place on
June 22, 1941, and installed a huge camp of
wooden barracks about two miles northwest
of Auschwitz. They tore down the village of
Brzezinka (*Birkenau* in German), and built the
camp on that site. The second camp was called
Auschwitz II. Around 15,000 Soviet prisoners
of war were held there. They all died.
Beginning in 1942, Jews from all over
occupied Europe were also sent to Auschwitz.
The huge gas chambers-crematoria I described
were built there, too.

You rattle off the names of these concentration camps and then you say that Birkenau wasn't really one. What do you mean?

We often confuse concentration camps and
the places where Jews were murdered. I told
you that Berthe was deported. The term
"deportee" is used in France for everyone the
Nazis sent to camps in Germany or Poland.
We would say that a baby arrested in the Vél
d'Hiv round-up was deported. We would use
the same word to describe what happened to
General Charles de Gaulle's niece who

belonged to a resistance group. She was deported to Ravensbruck. The word "deportee" was also used throughout the nineteenth century to refer to people sentenced to prison for political reasons.

Then what made some camps different?

The big difference is what happened when people arrived. The vast majority of Jews were sent to places, sometimes called camps, for the sole purpose of being put to death. Raul Hilberg, an important American historian, prefers not to use the terms "camp," "death camp" or "extermination camp" to refer to these places. He uses "killing centers." I think he's right. The first killing center opened in December 1941 at Chelmo in Poland, which the Nazis renamed Kulmhof. Three others followed: Belzec, Sobibor and Treblinka. We almost never talk about them because there were practically no survivors to provide testimony or tell us what happened there. The Nazis brought millions and millions of men, women, and children—probably 2.7 million people—by train to those places, just to gas them. Then they buried the bodies in pits or burned them in the crematories. They didn't need large facilities or many barracks because these places weren't intended to hold prisoners for very long. However, two camps, Majdanek and Auschwitz-Birkenau, were both concentration camps *and* killing centers. Prisoners went back and forth between Auschwitz and Birkenau so it's hard to make a clear distinction, but Auschwitz was primarily a concentration camp and Birkenau, a killing center.

Why do people talk mostly about Auschwitz?

There are several reasons why Auschwitz is the best-known camp. First, because the number of deaths were higher there than anywhere else. And second, although it might seem slightly contradictory, because there were more survivors, whether resistance members from various countries or Jews. After they were liberated, the survivors created important organizations that provided a lot of information about their experiences.

The concentration camps were terrifying places. For the most part, people arrived at the camps in the same way, much like Berthe did—with one exception: Auschwitz is the only camp where prisoners had a number tattooed in their flesh.

Prisoners suffered from hunger and cold. They were often forced to perform exhausting, even deadly, work in quarries or factories. They endured extreme humiliation. In the beginning, it was Germans who were held in the camps. They included Nazi opponents and Jehovah's Witnesses who refused to renounce their faith or give the Nazi salute. Later, men who refused to go to the army and women who would not work in the war industries were imprisoned. Homosexuals were, too.

Death rates during the war years ranged from one out of every four prisoners in the less harsh camps, like Buchenwald, to one out of every two in the worst, like Mauthausen. But even if death rates in the camps were shocking, we can't say that the goal of internment in those camps was extermination pure and simple.

You say that 2.7 million died from poison gas. The number I usually hear is six million.

The number six million includes the total number of Jews killed by gas and all other methods. Historians don't agree. Some say the number is five million. Others say seven.

When the number of deaths is so huge, it's very hard to give exact figures.

We're not talking just about Auschwitz any longer, although its name is often used to symbolize the destruction of the Jews of Europe. And because this is the darkest episode in the history of the twentieth century, Auschwitz also symbolizes the greatest evil that humans can do to each other.

People talk about genocide, too.

You're right. That's a fairly new word. Raphael Lemkin, a professor of international law who emigrated from Poland to the U.S, invented it in 1944. It refers specifically to the extermination of the Jews. The word comes from the Greek work *genos,* the race, and the Latin verb, *coedere,* to kill. It refers to the attempt to destroy an entire people.

And what about holocaust?

In the U.S. they use only the word "holocaust," but I don't like it. It means sacrifice by fire. That could give people the impression that the Jews sacrificed themselves, or were sacrificed, to God. In 1985, the French filmmaker Claude

Lanzmann produced a strange masterpiece in which he filmed survivors and witnesses, sometimes right at the spot where people died. He takes a very matter-of-fact approach and the result is that the viewer comes away with an even deeper understanding of the destruction of the Jews. It's almost 10 hours long and when you're older, you've got to see it. Lanzmann took the title of the movie from a Hebrew word, *shoah,* which means destruction. Shoah is another name for the genocide of the Jews, but it's not limited to Auschwitz.

You've just explained that the word genocide was invented to refer to what happened to the Jews in Nazi Europe. But I often hear it used when people talk about other events. Are they right?

That's a very tough question. Philosophers, historians, and even politicians have heated arguments on this subject, which is completely normal. Rafael Lemkin, the law professor I mentioned, gives genocide a legal definition and uses it in the context of international law. Since 1948, the United Nations has held that genocide violates international law.

For historians, the word itself isn't so important. We're more concerned with understanding what happened in the past. Let's say we define genocide as the will of a government, or some part of that government, to destroy a whole group of people. Even using that definition, it can be difficult to identify the decision to commit genocide or the person who made that decision. But I think two other events in twentieth century history qualify as genocide: the 1915 massacre of the Armenians by the Turks during World War I and the Hutus' recent slaughter of the Tutsis in Rwanda.

Going back to the war, were the Jews the only ones marked for death?

Jews weren't the only people to die in the gas chambers. Under the Third Reich, gypsies were interned in all the concentration camps and ghettos. They were sent to the killing centers, too. In 1942, a "family camp" was opened in Birkenau. Around 20,000 people were held there, in family groups, in thirty-two barracks. On the night of August 1, 1944, all of them—men, women, and children— were sent to the gas chambers.

How did people die if they weren't killed in the gas chambers?

The genocide of the Jews, or as the Nazis called it, the "final solution to the Jewish problem," didn't stop at Auschwitz or the killing centers.

What else happened?

I've already told you about the Nazis' first goal concerning the Jews: to make them disappear from the Third Reich. In the beginning, that meant forcing them to leave. From 1933 to 1939, Jews could leave Germany, Austria, or annexed Czechoslovakia by abandoning their property. The biggest problem for the Jews who left was finding a country that would take them in. The U.S. had closed its doors after the end of World War I. During the 1930s, Europe was devastated by economic crisis. One after another, every country closed its doors to immigration. By 1939, only one place would accept Jews: Shanghai, China's biggest city! After that, the Jews were trapped.

From the beginning of the war, the Germans dreamed of creating a place, like an Indian reservation, for Jews. They first thought of the island of Madagascar, which was then a

French colony. If a peace treaty had been signed with France, the Germans would have deported around 4 million Jews to Madagascar under SS guard. But there was no treaty. After Poland was invaded in September, 1939, they thought about creating a reservation near Lublin, in Nisko, Poland. They began deporting Jews there. Conditions were so horrible that people died by the hundreds. But after February 1941, Jews were forbidden to leave the Reich.

So they couldn't flee any longer?

When the German army invaded Poland, 3 million Jews fell under their control. Jews made up 10 percent of the Polish population, but in some cities and towns they represented nearly half. In places where they were in the majority, they hadn't assimilated like Jews in Germany or France. They were what we call a "national minority." That meant that at least in principle, Jews had certain rights, like the right to teach school in their language, Yiddish. There were lots of political parties representing them on town councils or in the national parliament. Then all of a sudden the Germans set up ghettos.

What's a ghetto?

Today the word is used to identify urban minority neighborhoods where living conditions are harsh, like New York's South Bronx. France has cities with minority neighborhoods, too, where poor people live. But the Polish ghettos looked like something out of the Middle Ages. These were areas totally shut off from the rest of the city. The Germans forced the Jews to live there, separated from the rest of the "Aryan"—non-Jewish—city by barbed wire. The biggest ghetto, in Warsaw, Poland, was actually walled off from the rest of the city. The Germans forced people from small towns to move to ghettos in the big cities and cram in there. Then they deported German Jews and gypsies and sent them to the ghettos. The Jews had to set up the ghettos as if they were little nations, but they had nothing.

How were the ghettos organized?

They were governed by Jewish councils, known as *Judenrat*. The Germans ordered the Jews to choose people to lead the councils, which were responsible for housing and feeding ghetto residents, finding work for people and keeping the ghetto clean. The ghettos had their own police, and the councils relied on them to carry out German orders. Some Jewish leaders who became *Judenrat* presidents were carried away by their own power. Chaim Rumkowski, the president in Lodz, Poland, acted as if he'd been appointed king of the Jews. He even minted coins with his picture. But he was an exception. Others believed they could use their power to save some Jews by making them work for the Germans. They thought the Jews' work would be so important that the Germans would decide to keep them alive.

It was an impossible situation. What should they have done? Leave people to face the Nazis on their own? Try to minimize the horrors of life in the ghetto, or more accurately, of survival in the ghetto? Some accused the people who participated in the *Judenrat* of collaborating with the Germans in exterminating their own people.

Is that what happened?

If you think about it, you realize that once the noose was tightened around the Jews, there was almost nothing that could have been done. The Jewish leaders faced an impasse. No matter what they did, they would have been guilty one way or another. In the end, there was no solution because everyone was going to die.

The Germans made sure that living conditions in the ghettos were awful. In 1941, for example, about 550,000 people were crammed into the Warsaw ghetto's 1½ square miles. At least 15 people lived in every apartment, with six, seven or more to a room. The Germans allowed only small amounts of food into the ghettos. Hunger was widespread. Typhus, an often-fatal disease spread by fleas, was epidemic. Between January 1941 and July 1942, 61,000 people died in the Warsaw ghetto alone. All together, 600,000 died of hunger in the ghettos. Every day, you'd see shrunken, wasted corpses in the streets.

Still, ghetto life did have some structure. Activists in local associations, often connected to political parties, set up community and refugee centers, orphanages, and cafeterias. People attended secret religious services. There were libraries, theaters, and even a clandestine medical school. Thanks to the black market, some people became rich and went out to nightclubs.

How do we know so much about what it was like to live in the ghetto?

Thanks to something unique in history: people who were locked up in them wrote about their experiences and saved everything they could. Chaim Kaplan, a teacher, was held in the Warsaw ghetto. He died there. He explained why, in spite of the danger, he kept a journal. "I am deeply convinced that we are living through an important time and that I have a responsibility and duty to history which I may not shirk," he wrote. "My diary will be a source for future historians."

Emmanuel Ringblum, a young historian, was also locked up. He organized teams responsible for collecting every document produced in the ghetto. He put these archives in metal cans and buried them. After the war, they were dug up from the ruins of the Warsaw ghetto.

You seem to think this is very important. Why?

The Nazis wanted to erase every trace of an entire people from the earth. The historian Ignacy Schiper, who was killed in Majdanek, explained it clearly. "Everything depends on those who leave their testimony for the next generations, on those who will write the history of this time. History is usually written by the victors. Everything we know about people who were killed is based on what their killers wanted us to know. If our killers are victorious, if they are the ones to write the history of this war, our destruction will be presented as one of the most beautiful pages in the history of the world. Future generations will honor the courage of these crusaders. Every one of their words will be taken as Gospel truth. Then they will have been able to erase us entirely from the world's memory as if we had never existed, as if there had never been Polish Jews, never a Warsaw ghetto, never a Majdanek."

Even with the deaths in the ghettos and the gas chambers, I still don't see how you reach the number of 6 million killed.

People didn't die only in those places. During the June 1941 German invasion of the Soviet Union, the German Army, the *Wehrmacht,* killed huge numbers of Jews. Special commando units made up of SS members accompanied the German army. Their job was to kill Communist leaders and Jews because the Nazis hated both groups. To them, Communists—or Bolsheviks, to use the Nazis' word—and Jews were all the same.

But even then, the Nazis made a distinction between Jews and Communist leaders. Commandant Otto Ohlendorf, the head of a unit that killed 90,000 people, explained that while entire Jewish families were targets, when it came to Communists, only specific individuals were marked for death. "The order called for exterminating the entire Jewish population," he said, making clear that he "had not been informed that families of Soviet commissioners were being sought."

What exactly were these units supposed to do?

When they arrived in a village, they brought all the Jews together in the center of the community. Then they led them to an isolated spot outside the village where several pits had been dug. Abraham Aviel, his family's only survivor, tells what happened next. "They began leading the Jews toward the pits in rows, group by group. They ordered the Jews to undress and when they climbed up the slope, we heard gunshots. They fell into the pits. Women, children, family after family. Every family went together."

machines so they shifted from machine gun massacres, like those that at pits on the village outskirts, to mass death by gas in the Polish camps. As I said before, Jews were killed by gas for the first time in December 1941. At first, the gassing was carried out in converted trucks. The goal of this method was to distance the victim from the executioner, who no longer killed anyone with his own hands. He could maintain the illusion of innocence, of not having blood on his hands.

Was this the first time such methods were used?

Yes and no. Gas had already been used during a massive euthanasia campaign Hitler had unleashed. He had decided the mentally ill were too expensive to care for. Even worse, they might get pregnant and their babies could damage the Aryan race. Even before he came to power, mixed-raced people had been sterilized. They included the children of Germans and Senegalese, Africans who had occupied part of Germany along with the French Army after World War I. Hitler also ordered that mentally ill people he considered "unworthy of living" be killed. So political authorities had already made decisions about who would live and who would be erased from the planet. Recent research suggests that about 200,000 disabled people died secretly, most often in gas vans. The operation ended in 1941 when Catholic priests finally protested. It's worth noting that the men who ran the euthanasia operation also organized the first Jewish killing centers.

Did Hitler want to kill all the Jews from the moment he took power?

No, the turning point didn't come until sometime between the end of 1941 and the beginning of 1942. That's when European Jews began to be killed systematically. From then on, it was no longer a question of killing just the Jews who were nearby, in occupied Poland or the USSR, but Jews throughout Europe.

On January 20, 1942 Germany's high-ranking officials gathered in Wannsee, just outside Berlin, to discuss the "final solution to the Jewish problem." We know what happened because a transcript of that meeting exists. The following passage makes it all clear, even if the language is coded. The Nazis often spoke in code because all their conversations were supposed to be secret.

The transcript reads: "In the interest of accomplishing the final solution, the Jews, under authorized supervision, will be transferred to the East and put to work. They will be organized in large work brigades, separated by sex. Able-bodied Jews will be sent to areas requiring roadwork. A considerable portion of their numbers will be eliminated by natural causes. Those remaining alive should, by the very fact of their survival, be considered and treated as the most resistant, as they will be the product of natural selection. If released, they could constitute a seed for rebuilding the Jewish population."

What does that mean in ordinary language?

It means that the stronger ones, who manage to stay alive in spite of harsh conditions, must be eliminated by other means to prevent the rebirth of the Jewish people.

So it wasn't by accident that the round-up at the Vél d'Hiv took place in July 1942?

If you had to choose the worst month in the entire war, it would have to be July 1942. At practically the same time that the round-up was taking place, the SS was organizing the mass deportation of the Warsaw Jews, hoping to put pressure on Adam Czerniakow, the *Judenrat*'s leader. He kept a journal, too, in which he recorded the day's events in the ghetto. On July 22, 1942 he wrote, "We disconnected the telephone lines. The children were moved out of the little garden opposite. It was announced to us that with few exceptions, all Jews, without regard to sex or age, would be deported to the East. Today we must supply 6,000 souls by 4 o'clock. They will expect the same, if not more, every day."

The next day Czerniakow killed himself. He understood that what the Germans called "the transfer to the East" really meant death. He left his wife this note: "They are demanding that I kill the children of my people with my own hands."

So the deportation went ahead without the Judenrat's leader.

Even without Czerniakow, the ghetto emptied out as 5,000 to 7,000 people were deported every day. A train station had been set up at its edge. From there, trains left for the killing centers at Treblinka, around 75 miles from Warsaw. At the same time, other trains carrying human cargo left France, Holland, and Belgium and rolled toward Auschwitz. The deportation of the Warsaw Jews took seven weeks. We don't have an exact count but it's estimated that 265,000 to 310,000 Warsaw Jews were gassed when they arrived at Treblinka.

I still can't understand why they let themselves be taken away. Why didn't they fight?

Some say the Jews let themselves be carted away like sheep to the slaughter. That's a cruel thing to say about the dead. They don't deserve it. I know it seems impossible to imagine, but try to put yourself in that time. First, Jews didn't know the Nazis wanted to kill them all. They didn't know that the trains were taking them to the gas chambers. When the Nazis counted them, took their belongings—sometimes, as in France, with the help of governments collaborating with the Germans—and locked them in ghettos, like in Poland, the Jews didn't realize that a huge machine had been assembled to carry out all those steps. They certainly didn't know where all these events were headed. And even if they were worried, if rumors had reached them, they couldn't believe what they were hearing because it all seemed so unlikely and monstrous. Besides, how could they have known? The Germans themselves hadn't yet defined what they called the "Final Solution." As I explained, they had been planning to make the Reich *Judenrein,* cleansed of Jews, by moving the Jews out.

When did they decide that the "Final Solution" would be complete extermination?

Historians don't agree on the date because there is no written order from Hitler. Some say it was in June 1941, when the Soviet Union was invaded. Others point to what might be called a regional strategy: first, eliminate the Soviet Jews, then the Polish Jews, and finally, after the Wannsee conference, all the European Jews who might fall into Nazi hands. We do know that when the census of French Jews took place and the Warsaw Jews were locked in their walled ghetto, the Germans hadn't yet decided on extermination.

Today we know how the story ended, so we interpret each chapter as leading to that end. But if you'd been living back then, you couldn't know where it would all lead. There they were, day after day, without any information, without newspapers or radio. The rumors that reached them were full of contradictions. They could only imagine what might happen the next day. Today, for example, we know the census files would be used to arrest them. If they had known, would they have let themselves be counted? Answer that question for yourself.

What did people know then? Did information get around?

It's very hard to say what people knew at the time. A lot depended on where you lived. In Poland, for example, where the killing centers were located, news traveled fast but not as fast as people thought. In France, it probably moved more slowly. Men and women took great risks to pass along information. For example, thanks to leaks in the police department, many people were warned about the round-up at the Vél d'Hiv. The Germans had intended to arrest 30,000 Jews in two days. They managed to catch only 13,000, which was bad enough. Because only men had been arrested up to then, the women thought they and their children would be safe. That's why mostly women and children were taken.

But could people still escape the round-ups?

You could go underground, but it wasn't easy.
It depended on the country. In France, for
example, you had to get false documents and
pay a smuggler to take you across the line
separating the occupied zone from the free
zone. If you were a foreigner and spoke
French badly or had an accent, it was
especially dangerous. And most importantly,
you had to find food for yourself and your
family. The poorer you were, the less money
you had and the harder it was.

Still, many Jews survived with help from
other French people. Of the 330,000 Jews
living in France in 1939, around 75,000 were
deported and died. Berthe was among the
2,500 Jews from France who were deported to
Auschwitz but survived. So four out of five
Jews were saved. In Poland, where around
three million died, it was nearly impossible to
hide. The population was deeply anti-Semitic,
so the people there weren't about to protect
Jews. Like the Germans, Poles believed there
was a "Jewish problem." The Nazi solution
didn't upset many Poles who were themselves
harshly oppressed by the Nazis. The Poles
were upset by the Jews' presence in their
country. And in Poland, German law was
enforced more harshly than in France. If a

Polish Catholic hid a Jew and was discovered, he and everyone in his house would be executed on the spot.

In general, did Jews resist?

If you think about it, what's surprising is that some Jews were able to resist at all. Historians, who love to argue even when they agree on the facts, have spent a long time discussing exactly what resistance meant for the Jews. Some think we should take the word in its literal, physical sense: a force that opposes another force. For the Jews, resistance was simply the struggle to survive, to oppose the will to murder with the will to live. So in France, organizations like OSE (Children's Aid Society) made it possible to save children.

Because they were able to rescue children?

To rescue children, you had to get them false documents and find young women to take them to safe places, usually to families in the countryside or to convents. Some regions, like the Cevennes or the village of Chambon-sur-Lignon in the Massif Central, became true refuges for Jews. In Poland, the first calls for help were sent out only after the Warsaw Jews were deported in the summer of 1942.

Why was it harder to help the Polish Jews?

Not many Poles cared about saving Jews. In protest, a well-known Polish woman writer, Zofia Kossak-Szczucka, wrote, "Anyone who remains silent in the face of murder is an accomplice to murder. Anyone who does not condemn, approves." In Poland, the Jews were at a particular disadvantage. The German occupation was especially brutal. The leaders of Polish society were systematically imprisoned, sent to concentration camps, or executed. The Poles were in a very risky situation.

However, Jewish and Polish political leaders did form a committee to help Jews. It distributed money and helped 8,000 Jews hide by providing false documents, finding shelter—which was very difficult—and building hiding places in caves or behind false apartment walls. The committee managed to hide around 2,500 children in convents and 1,300 in Polish families. By comparison to the three million who died, these numbers are tiny. But we need to remember the very special and modest heroism of these men and women who just did their human duty.

During inhuman times, sometimes just being human is heroic.

Is that why the killing centers were all in Poland?

I don't think so. I think it was largely a practical matter. Lots of Jews lived near these places.

So for Jews, to resist meant surviving and helping others to survive?

Not just that. Some participated in armed Resistance movements. Your grandfather, Étienne, joined several armed groups in Grenoble and Lyon. They were part of immigrant resistance groups. He and his school friends weren't really foreigners because they were born in France and spoke French. They fought the Nazi occupiers by derailing trains and organizing attacks against the Germans.

But when we talk to him about that period, he always says he has one regret: that he didn't fight to save Jewish children from deportation. That's why now that he's retired, he doesn't spend much time on the history of the Resistance, but he works to make sure the deported Jewish children aren't forgotten. He helps place commemorative plaques on the walls of the schools they attended in Paris.

And what about resistance in Poland?

Some fought in the camps or in the ghettos, where a few revolts did take place. The most famous is the Warsaw rebellion. Remember that in the summer of 1942, the Nazis had emptied the ghetto of most of its residents. After the mass deportations, the ghetto had shrunk. Only 40,000 people were left. They worked in small factories for the German army.

The mood had changed. During deportation, everyone worried about their own survival and that of the people close to them. By the fall of 1942, everyone understood the awful truth. Deportation and "resettlement" in the East meant death. The idea of an armed resistance took shape. A young man, 24-year-old Mordechai Anieliewicz, became the leader of a new Jewish military organization. His friend Marek Edelmann, the last member of the group who is still alive, wrote, "He calculated the odds of this unequal combat. He knew that the ghetto and its businesses would be destroyed. He was convinced that neither he nor his fighters would survive the ghetto's liquidation. They would die homeless, like dogs, and no one would even know where they were buried."

How did they fight?

They needed weapons. The Polish resistance didn't trust them and gave them barely any arms. They received ten revolvers at first and then 49 more. That's barely 60 altogether. On January 18, 1943, the Germans entered the ghetto. They had decided to deport 8,000 Jews. But gunfire broke out in a column of soldiers escorting the deportees to the train station. Several Germans were killed and wounded. Other groups rose up suddenly throughout the ghetto and the Germans abandoned the round-ups. It was a victory for the Jewish armed resistance. As of that moment, the Germans knew the Jews wouldn't leave the ghetto voluntarily.

When the Germans decided to "liquidate" the Jews, to use their word, they organized as if preparing for battle. On April 19, 1943, at 2 A.M., guards and police surrounded the ghetto. At 5 A.M., small groups entered, stationing themselves at empty lots. At 7 A.M., they advanced in two tight columns, marching in step through streets that looked deserted.

Singing as they advanced, the soldiers in the first column were attacked. They retreated. The second column tried to take a position in the center of the ghetto. The resistance opened fire and the Germans fell back. Twelve Germans were killed or injured in that first attack. By 2 P.M., not a single German remained in the ghetto.

Combat resumed the next morning. The SS general in charge decided to change tactics, taking the ghetto houses one by one. But the combatants knew the ghetto like the back of their hands. They fired from roofs and shelters. With their weapons pointed down and white ribbons in their buttonholes, three German officers tried to negotiate a ceasefire to evacuate their dead and wounded soldiers. Imagine what that meant to the young combatants. A handful of starving civilians against the most powerful army in the world!

But in the end the Germans liquidated the ghetto!

Yes. On the third day, they infiltrated in small groups and set houses on fire using flame-throwers. Combat continued for two weeks. On May 8 they surrounded the headquarters of the Jewish resistance, located in a fortified underground shelter. No one wanted to surrender. Most committed suicide, including the leader, Mordechai Anieliewicz. On May 16, 1943, the SS general blew up the Warsaw synagogue and declared the end of the Jewish quarter. That's how the last of the 500,000 Jews who had been packed into the ghetto died.

So the ghetto was gone?

The Nazis weren't satisfied with killing all the Jews. They had to erase every sign of the Jews' presence. In July 1943, they built a small concentration camp on the site of the ghetto and moved about 3,000 Auschwitz prisoners into it. The prisoners' job was to gather property other Jews had left behind and to clear the ruins. No trace of the ghetto was to remain. The place where Jews had lived for centuries would be replaced by a park.

From a military point of view, if you compare the Warsaw ghetto insurrection with huge battles like the one at Stalingrad, in the former Soviet Union, it's only a footnote to history. But even though it ended with death, it's a powerful symbol of resistance.

You spoke of regular people who helped Jews.
What about the big powers, the allies?
Didn't they do anything?

Today we know that the allies, especially
Churchill and Roosevelt, were aware of what
was happening, especially in Poland. They got
their information from different sources.
Couriers from the Polish Resistance brought
information to London. The representative of
the World Jewish Congress in Geneva told
them exactly what was happening in the
killing centers. But for various reasons, the
allies couldn't or wouldn't do anything to save
the Jews.

What were their reasons?

First of all, no one wanted to take people into
their country. And then, given their objective,
which was to win the war, they didn't want
any distractions. They simply thought that
when the allies had won, the Jews would be
liberated like everyone else!

Were they wrong?

Yes and no, because there were really two wars. In one, nations and their respective armies fought against each other. The other was the Nazis' war against the Jews, which was carried on inside the world war. When Hitler understood he was losing the world war, he could still celebrate because there would be no more Jews in Europe. Despite all the military intelligence they received, the allies refused to face that fact. Not the Soviets, not the Americans, none of them. It just wasn't their problem.

When did they finally understand?

When the allied armies entered Germany, they discovered, accidentally, the concentration camps and the state of the survivors—skeletons with sunken eyes.

They discovered the camps by accident?

Yes. They knew about the old, prewar camps. News had filtered out during the war. But even so, the allied armies didn't expect they would be liberating people interned in camps.

No one had anticipated what kind of shape the internees might be in. Indeed, people kept dying even after liberation because no one made sure they were fed properly. For a short time, the Americans and the English encouraged the press to report on the horrors of the concentration camps.

Concentration camps? You told me concentration camps and genocide weren't the same.

You're right. It took people a long time to become aware that this was genocide. The first important event was Adolf Eichmann's 1961 trial in Jerusalem. Before the war, Eichmann oversaw the forced emigration of Jews from Austria and Prague. During the war, he was in charge of deportations. After the war, he managed to hide and then moved secretly to Argentina. The Israeli secret service found him and took him to Jerusalem, where he was put on trial. The trial was gripping. It lasted months. More than 100 survivors testified about every stage of genocide. You could say that the world finally realized then—15 years later—what Auschwitz was. Only then did people understand the fate that had been reserved just for the Jews.

You say that Eichmann was put on trial. Was he the only guilty one? Sometimes you talk about Germans, sometimes about Nazis. . . .

As soon as the Allies won the war, the four victorious allied nations (the U.S., Great Britain, the former Soviet Union, and France) organized a massive criminal proceeding known as the Nuremberg trial. About twenty of the highest-ranking Nazi officials were put on trial. At that time, the allies were occupying Germany and many trials were held there. At the time, people referred to this as "denazification," which meant removing all former Nazis from important government positions. No one said much about what had been done to the Jews. But when Eichmann went on trial, the crimes committed against Jews in the East, the USSR, and Poland began to be discussed. Judicial proceedings began.

Recently a scandal broke out regarding an exhibit on German army crimes. For a long time, the Germans put the Nazis and the *Wehrmacht,* the German Army, in two separate categories. Here's what they would say: the Nazis were responsible for mass killings, especially of Jews. The *Wehrmacht,* with its proud Prussian tradition, was free of Nazi ideology and followed the rules of war. It was an army like any other. But this exhibit showed that the regular army also participated in mass killings.

So are all Germans from that time guilty?

People asked themselves that after the war. We're still asking the same question today. There is no such thing as collective guilt. Germans who opposed Nazism were persecuted, interned in concentration camps, and forced into exile. Like many other European countries, Germany was deeply anti-Semitic even if the active, murderous anti-Semites were only a minority. It's estimated that around 100,000 Germans took an active part in genocide.

But what can we say about the others, the ones who watched their Jewish neighbors being arrested? The ones who drove the deportation trains? The vast majority of Germans were completely indifferent. That's what's most shocking.

What did the Jews do to make people want to kill them all?

Nothing! When someone is the victim of a crime, we often ask the wrong question: what did he or she do wrong? We suspect it's the victim's fault. It may sound bizarre, but even the innocent victim often feels guilty. That's not unusual in rape cases, for example. Some say that the woman was more or less responsible for what happened to her. They're wrong. The Nazis didn't hold the Jews responsible for doing something wrong. The fact that they were Jewish was all that mattered.

Why were they anti-Semitic?

Anti-Semitism is ancient. Some say it dates back 3,000 years to the birth of Judaism. Others think it originates in Christianity. That would mean we'd call it anti-Judaism. Jews were criticized for not accepting Jesus as the Messiah, rejecting the "good news" that Jesus is Christ, and refusing to be converted to Christianity.

Even worse, Jews were accused of killing Christ. For 2,000 years, every generation of Jews has been blamed, again and again, for his death. Christian anti-Judaism emerged during the Middle Ages and fed all kinds of myths, according to which Jews were demonic and linked to the devil. When the black plague raged in Europe, Jews were supposed to have poisoned the wells. They were accused of ritual murders. Every year at Passover, Jews were said to kill a Christian child to mix his blood into the *matzoh,* the unleavened Passover bread.

Yet even then, during the massacres committed during the Crusades, Jews could escape by converting to Christianity. Those who refused to give up their beliefs were considered martyrs who sacrificed their lives for the sanctification of God's name.

I don't see the connection to Nazi Germany. Did this medieval anti-Judaism last that long?

Although the hatred of Jews that emerged at the end of the nineteenth century did resemble Christian anti-Judaism, it was new, like the word invented in Germany to describe it: anti-Semitism. As I explained, western European Jews had been emancipated. They participated in economic and social life in the countries where they lived. In Germany, there were only around 500,000 Jews, barely one percent of the population. But many were well-educated and had chosen fields that Protestants or Catholics had abandoned, including journalism, theater, medicine, and even politics.

Germany was modernizing rapidly during that period. Some intellectuals feared change would weaken German civilization. They wanted to protect their idea of the German Nation, which they said should include only Aryans. Jews were seen as foreigners who corrupted and weakened Germany.

Anti-Semitism increased after Germany lost World War I. Times were hard. The Germans were humiliated by the terms of the Peace Treaty of Versailles. Unemployment was high and the cost of food skyrocketed. Money lost its value. Jews were accused of having caused all these bad things. Germany saw itself as the victim of an international Jewish conspiracy.

Even if German anti-Semitism doesn't completely explain the genocide of the Jews, and if Hitler's anti-Semitism was different because he intended to save civilization by exterminating the Jews, it was still an important factor.

But anti-Semitism doesn't exist today.

It's true that in a country like France, for example, anti-Semitism can't be expressed publicly. It's against the law, as are racist demonstrations. But anti-Semitism isn't always easy to identify. According to a small group of people called revisionists, the gas chambers never existed. These people are out of touch with reality. A larger group says the chambers were only a minor detail of World War II. But it's easy to see that their real motivation is anti-Semitism. If Auschwitz hadn't happened, then it would be easy to be anti-Semitic again.

It's really painful to hear this. We're in a new millennium. Even if anti-Semitism appears sometimes, Jews aren't really persecuted any more. But I often hear people say, "We must never forget." Do you think this time in history deserves a special place?

When you drew your family tree, you learned that you have relatives who died in Auschwitz. Although we can visit the cemetery where your maternal grandfather, Aby, and your paternal grandmother, Anna, are buried, some of your great-grandparents have no grave. Paul Celan, the great German poet, wrote, "You'll have a grave in the clouds."

We must remember their names. We must hold onto every trace of them because everyone comes from the people who came before. Everyone has a history. I hope that when your children draw their family tree, they'll be able to write the names of their great-great-grandparents as well as the place where they died: Auschwitz.

So this is relevant only to families whose relatives died in Auschwitz?

No. It's not just a family matter. It's not even an event that concerns only Jews. Auschwitz is part of European history. If you think about it, it's probably the most European of all events in the entire history of the twentieth century! The story is still alive because some Auschwitz survivors, like Berthe, are still here. However, it's moving farther and farther away from us. It's becoming history. But just as people learn their family history, they need to learn about the world they come from.

Why should we study *this* particular historical episode? Some people think that knowing about what happened at Auschwitz will prevent it from happening again. That's what some said about World War I. It was supposed to be "the war to end all wars." It's as if by showing youth how people suffered during war, we can inoculate them against even thinking about committing such horrible acts themselves.

I'm skeptical about those pronouncements. I don't think that an historical account based on emotion alone can have lasting effects. I still believe in reason and the value of intelligence, even if we can't explain Auschwitz. And the genocide of the Jews was such an unprecedented event that it offers infinite opportunities to study and reflect on every aspect of human life and history. That's why people talk about it so much.

Take international affairs, for example. Since World War II, people have thought a lot about how to prevent crimes like those committed against the Jews. That's led to advances in the law. Today, efforts are underway to create a permanent international court of justice to try cases of crimes against humanity.

Other attitudes are changing. After World War II, all nations agreed that actions taken inside one country's borders—like building concentration camps, killing members of minority groups or forcing them to leave—were internal political matters. But there is growing support for outside intervention in other nations' internal affairs. When people think about these questions, they remember the great powers' inaction and indifference toward the Jews.

Studying genocide also helps us think about how modern nations work. Without people colluding at every step, Jews couldn't have been deported and put to death in gas chambers. Bureaucrats had to assemble files, police had to arrest Jews, and more bureaucrats had to organize and guard the camps. Someone had to drive the buses to the trains and drive the trains to the killing centers. Someone else had to make up the train schedules. But no one could see how each individual's job represented a link in the chain that, in the end, allowed millions of people to die. No single person did anything wrong. They all just did their jobs.

Of course, this doesn't apply to Himmler or Eichmann. They knew exactly what they were doing. And none of this would have been possible without the backdrop of the war. But even if many people didn't necessarily support what was happening, they couldn't, wouldn't, or didn't know how to resist.

Maurice Papon, a high-ranking official in the collaborationist Vichy government of wartime France, signed documents authorizing the deportation of Jews from Bordeaux. In 1997, during Papon's trial for crimes against humanity, people talked about "bureaucratic crimes." Sometimes all it takes to send people to their death is for a bureaucrat to follow instructions from a superior and just sign a simple form. And then there's the indifference we see all the time, like the neighbor who doesn't want to get involved any more than a powerful country does.

These questions will always haunt me. As an historian and teacher, I hope I can shed some light on them. I think they are important ones that every person should take time to think about.